TASKS AND AIMS

Photography has become an indispensable and outstanding means of propaganda in the revolutionary class struggle.

Thirty or forty years ago, the bourgeoisie already understood that a photograph has a very special effect on the viewer. For an illustrated book is easier to read and more likely to be bought, and an illustrated paper is a more entertaining read than the lead article of a political daily. Photography works on the human eye; what is seen is reflected in the brain without forcing the viewer into complicated thought. In this way the

The worker photographer movement mainly existed in the interwar period, related to the various national communist parties, under the leadership of the 3rd International. This is the first extensive presentation in any language of some of its activities. There are gaps — we have little or, as yet, no information on established groups in, for example, Austria, Czechoslovakia, France, Japan, Rumania, Scandinavia, Switzerland and the USSR! But we hope to publish more material on them in future annuals.

Translation: Sylvia Gohl

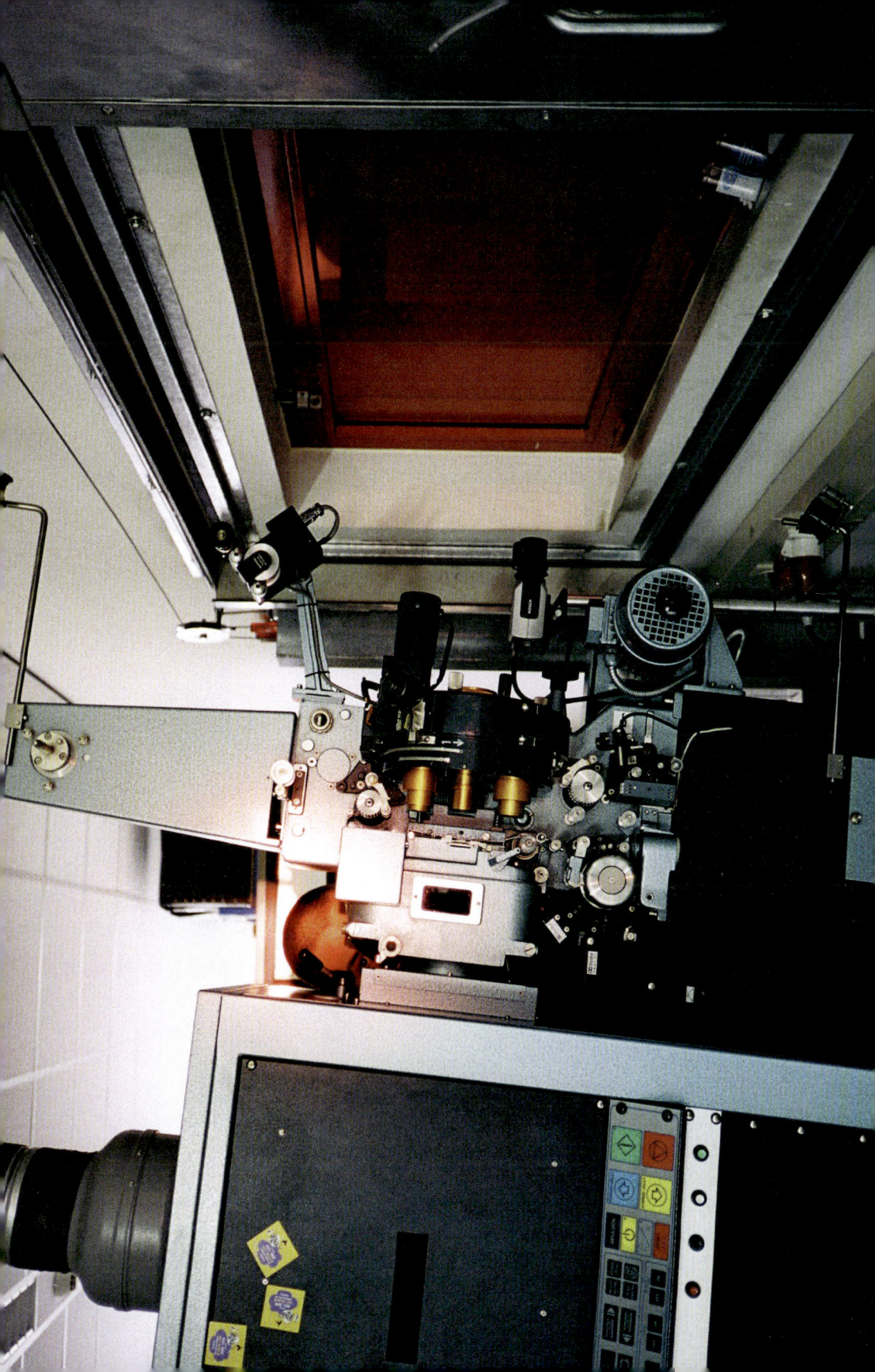

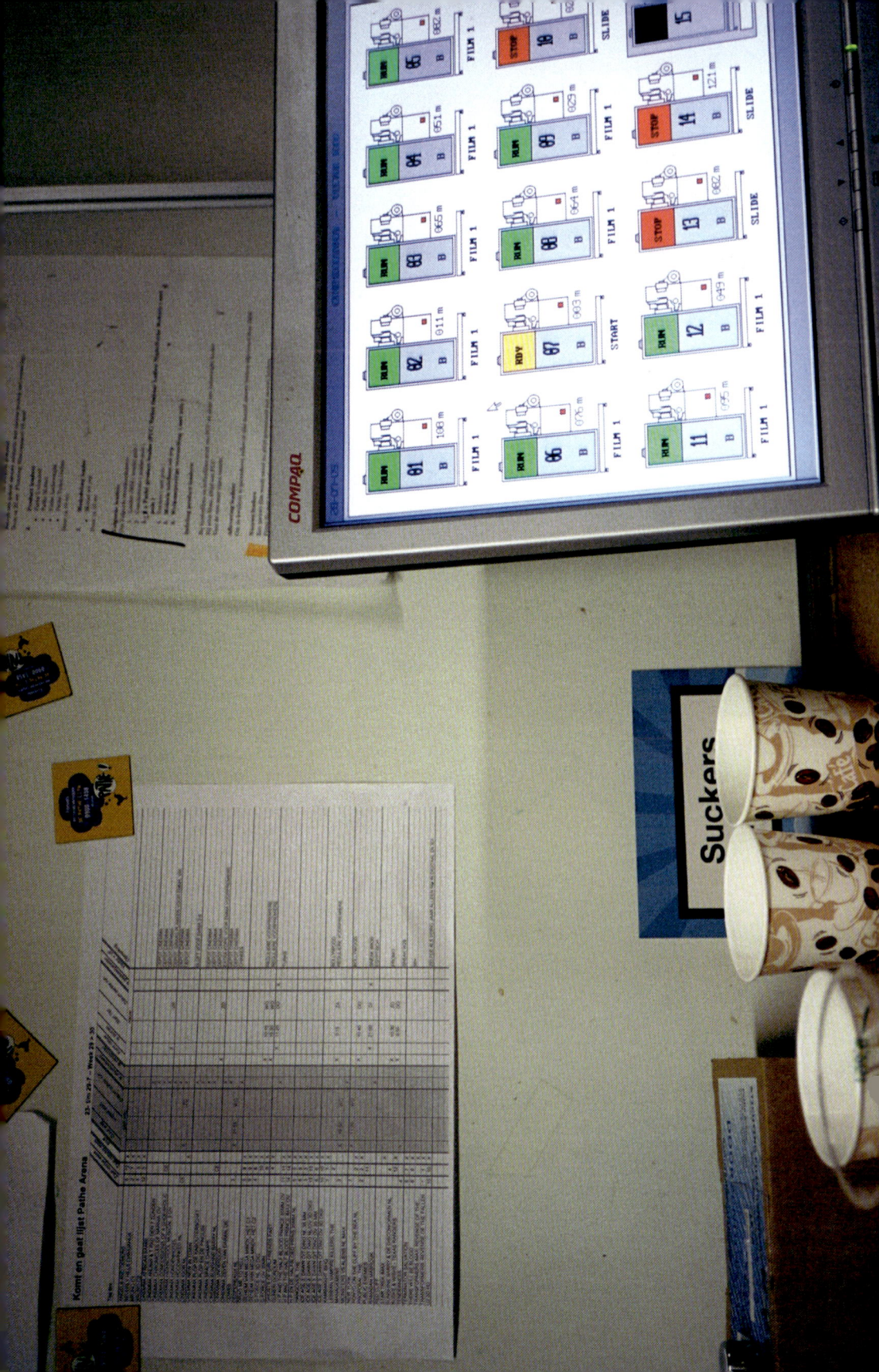

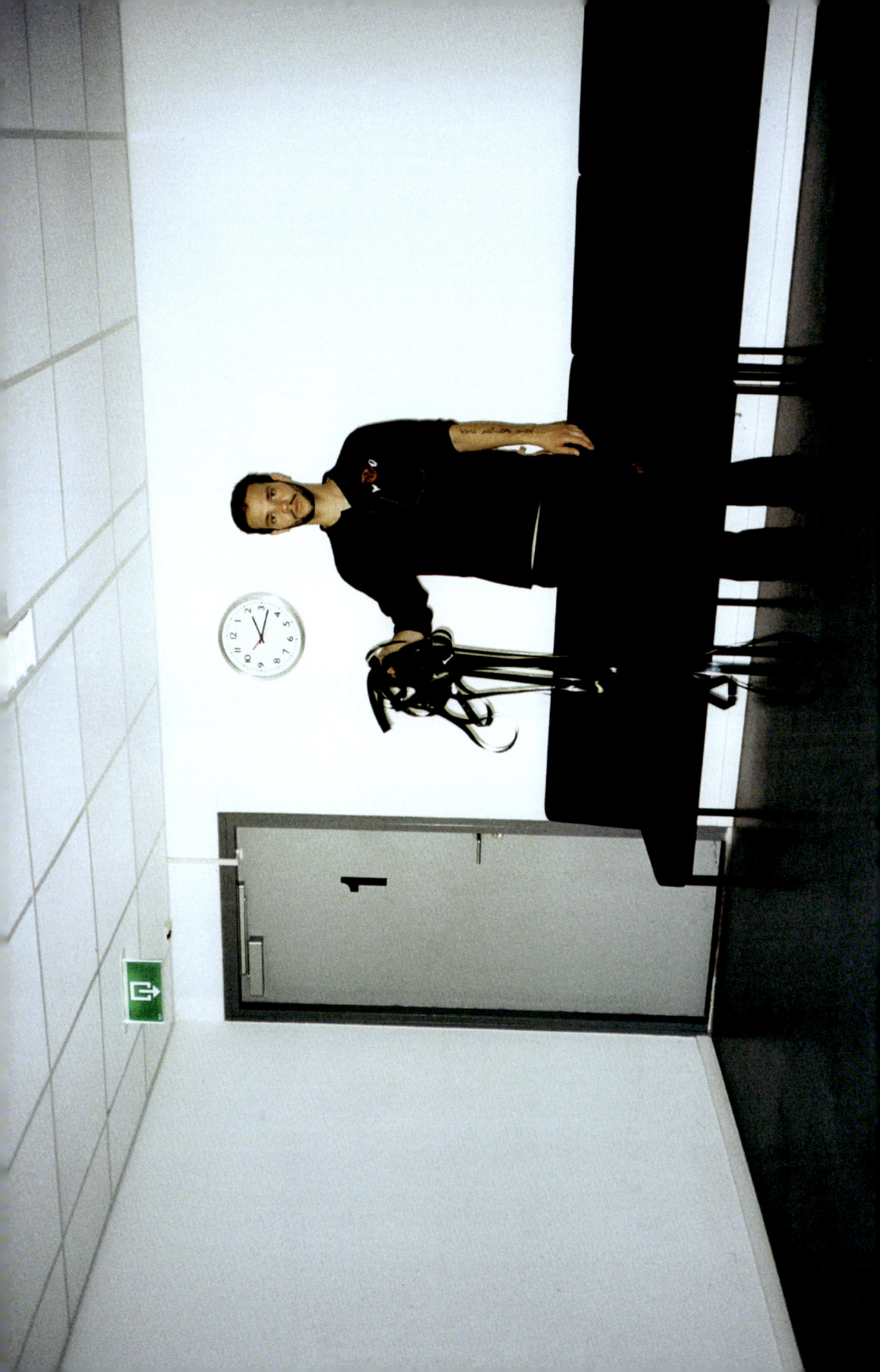

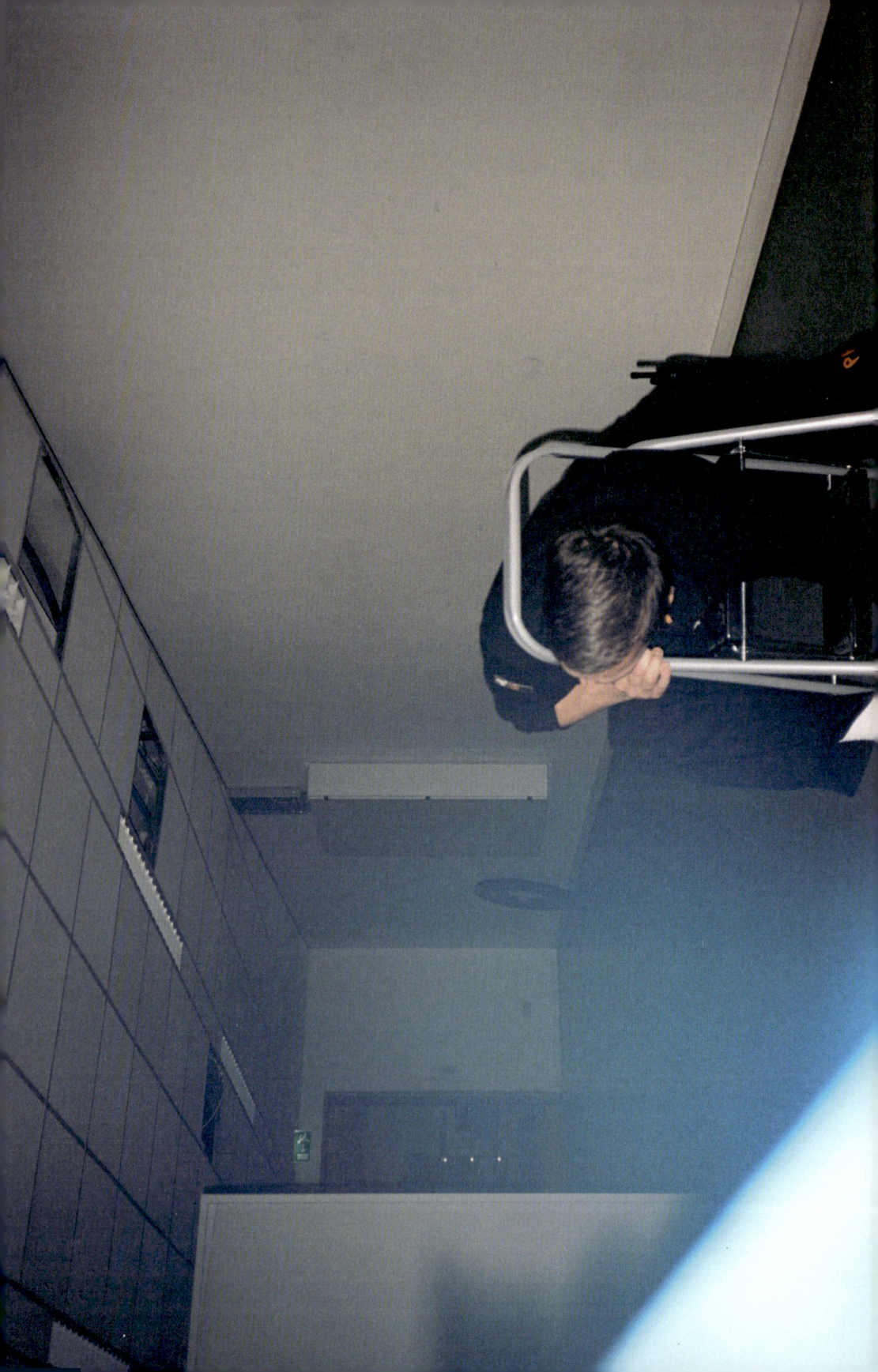

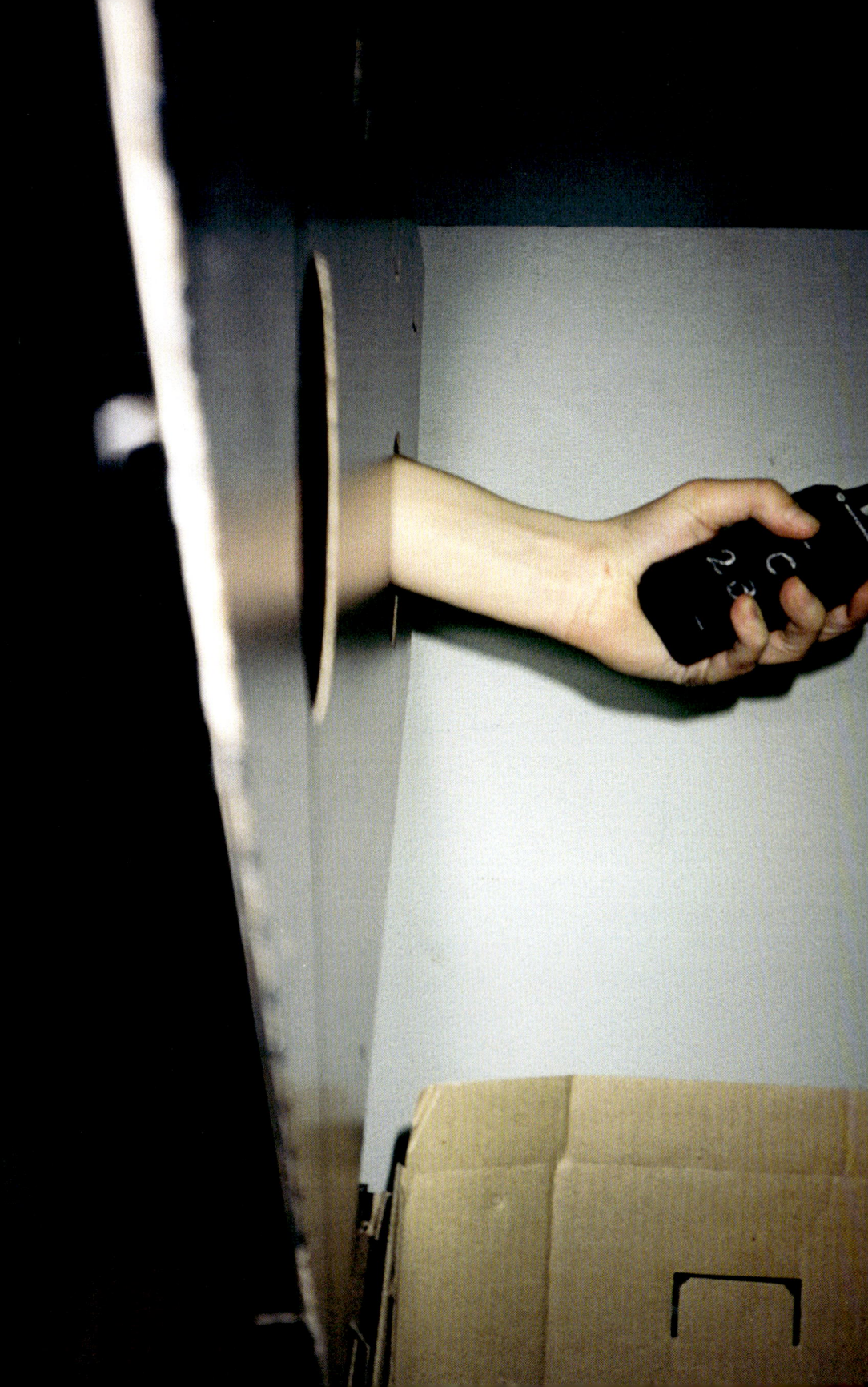

effect which is achieved by the juxtaposition of several pictures, by captions and accompanying texts. That is the decisive point. In this way a skilful editor can falsify every photograph into its opposite, and can influence the politically naive reader in any way he chooses.

The revolutionary workers of all countries have to realize these facts very clearly. They have to fight the class enemy with all means, have to beat him on all fronts. Just as the workers of the Soviet Union have learnt to make their own machine-tools, to invent things themselves to be put into the service of peaceful socialist construction, and just as workers in capitalist countries have learnt to write their own newspapers, so the proletarian amateur photographers have to learn to master the camera and to use it correctly in the international class struggle.

Willi Munzenberg, Der Arbeiter-Fotograf, 1931.

source: photography/politics one
photography workshop (1979),
london, united kingdom.